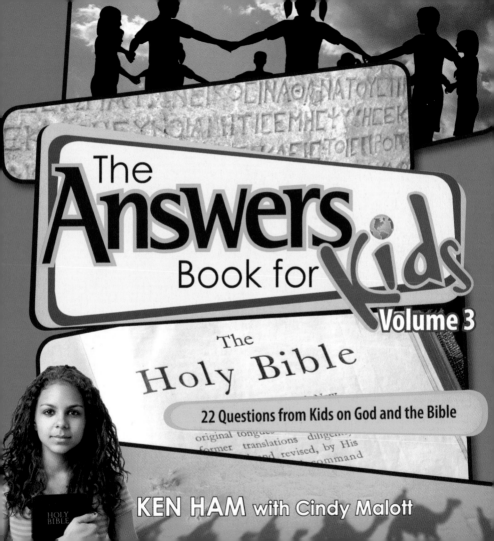

The
Answers
Book for Kids

Volume 3

The
Holy Bible

22 Questions from Kids on God and the Bible

original tongues
former translations diligently
and revised, by His
command

KEN HAM with Cindy Malott

Second Printing: September 2009

Master Books®
P.O. Box 726
Green Forest, AR 72638

Printed by L.E.G.O. SpA in Vicenza, Italy.

Book design by Terry White

ISBN 10: 0-89051-525-5
ISBN 13: 978-0-89051-525-9
Library of Congress Control Number: 2009900147

All Scripture references are New King James Version unless otherwise noted.

Please visit our website for other great titles: www.masterbooks.net

When you see this icon, there will be related Scripture references noted for parents to use in answering their children's, and even their own, questions.

For Parents and Teachers

Therefore whoever hears these sayings of Mine, and does them, I will liken him to a wise man who built his house on the rock: and the rain descended, the floods came, and the winds blew and beat on that house; and it did not fall, for it was founded on the rock (Matthew 7:24-25).

Dear Moms and Dads:

When I think of my father's memorial service and the individual testimonies of each of his six children, I am reminded of the tremendous legacy he left us. In different words and styles, each of us conveyed the same basic theme: Dad always stood up for what he believed, he taught his children to love the Word of God, and he always insisted that the authority of God's Word takes precedence over the fallible words of man. My dad's favorite book was his personal Bible—he loved it. It is well-worn and his study notes appear throughout it.

His words, life, and example demonstrated to me that the only foundation necessary to withstand life's many storms is the knowledge of God through His Word.

You, too, are leaving a legacy to the children in your life. Is your love for the Bible shaping them and the way they look at the world? I pray that this little book will equip you to lead your children to God's Word to find the answers to the questions they have. And that one day, by the power of His Word, they will repent of their sins and claim Jesus Christ as their Lord and Savior. To God be the glory!

Ken Ham
President/CEO, Answers in Genesis

3

Question:

I don't know if I believe in God because, I mean, who made God anyway?

Jason W.

Age 11 — Alabama, USA

4

Answer:

I am the Alpha and the Omega, the Beginning and the End," says the Lord, "who is and who was and who is to come, the Almighty" (Revelation 1:8).

Well, Jason, a lot of very smart people have asked this question. After all, if everything has a beginning or is made out of something or had a creator, then people think God must have had one too! So, let's think about it. If someone made God, then you must have a bigger God who made that God . . . and a bigger, bigger God who made that bigger God who made God. . . then a bigger, bigger, bigger God who made the bigger, bigger God who made the bigger God who made God. You see, Jason, we could go on and on and on. The only thing that makes sense is we have to have the biggest God of all. God—the God of the Bible—is the Creator of everything. Nothing and no one is bigger than Him. He was not created but has always existed. He is the Alpha (beginning) and Omega (end). The Bible says, "In the beginning, God created the heavens and the earth." In the beginning God was already there and He created all things to teach us more about Him and to show us His power, His goodness, and His wisdom.

Genesis 1:1; Psalm 19:1; Revelation 4:11

5

Question: What does God look like?

Calista M.

Age 8 — New Hampshire, USA

6

Answer:

. . . who alone has immortality, dwelling in unapproachable light, whom no man has seen or can see, to whom be honor and everlasting power. Amen (1 Timothy 6:16).

How wonderful it will be to finally see God in all His glory. We read that God lives in light so bright that we could never come near it, and that He is a spirit. When the prophet Ezekiel described his vision of God, he included bright fire, flashes of lightning, even the brightness of a rainbow in a cloud on a rainy day. But we are ALL sinners and the Bible says because of this, we are blind to spiritual things. We are born sinners because of Adam's disobedience in the Garden of Eden. And we can't see God because of our sinfulness. So while we are here on earth, we cannot see Him, we cannot know what He looks like, even though He is present with us. However, we see the glory of God in the face of Jesus Christ as revealed in the Bible. Now there is good news. God loved us and He had a plan that would save us. Jesus Christ stepped into history as a man, died on a cross, and rose from the dead. He promises that everyone who believes in Him, who calls on His name, who is sorry for his or her sins, and receives His free gift of forgiveness and salvation, will one day be with Him in heaven—where we will finally see our holy, merciful God.

Ezekiel 1; Romans 3:23; John 4:24; John 3:16; 2 Corinthians 4:6

Question: Where is God? Why can't I see him?

Rachael S.

Age 6 — Ohio, USA

8

Answer:

But He said, "You cannot see My face; for no man shall see Me, and live" (Exodus 33:20).

We can't see God because He is a spirit—but the Bible says Moses spoke to God face to face! Can we see God like Moses? The Bible tells us He is omnipresent by His Spirit. That means He is everywhere and sees everything all the time. That is very hard to understand, and seems simply amazing, even to me! I get a tiny idea of just how amazing it is when I fly in an airplane (which I do quite a bit). When I go over a big city like Los Angeles or New York and I look down I see thousands and thousands of lights—cars, houses, buildings, shopping malls, lots of people down there. I realize that God sees them at soccer, at the mall, in the house, at church, in the park, playing with their friends, He sees EVERYONE and KNOWS what they are doing! He also knows our hearts. He knows what we are thinking. He knows whether we love Him. He knows our needs. He is everywhere, Rachael, and He knows everything about you. And even though we accept this by faith, it is not a blind faith. You see, what we read in God's Word, which is the primary way God communicates to us today, makes sense of what we see in God's world. Also, in many ways, science confirms God's Word is true. Now God revealed Himself to us in the person of Jesus—when He came to earth as a man. And Rachael, lots of eyewitnesses saw Jesus and the miracles He did! Today we "see Him" through the words of the Bible.

Psalm 139:1-6; John 4:24; 2 Chronicles 16:9

Question: How big is God?

Jemima F.

Age 10 — Northern Ireland

10

Answer:

"...Do I not fill heaven and earth?" says the LORD (Jeremiah 23:24).

We already touched on this in question one, but let's look at it a different way. We tend to think of things in terms of a physical size. For example, we can look at how tall people are, how big the dog is, how high the mountains are, how wide the creek is—you get the idea. We compare the things we see when it comes to size. Some things are very big and some things are very small. But God doesn't have a physical form. Remember? God is spirit and He fills both time and space because He is spirit. We know that God created the universe. (Now that is very big!) And there sure isn't anything in the whole universe we can compare Him to. So, when we talk about how big God is we need to understand that God is infinite. (Infinite means we can't even measure it and there are no words to describe it—it is forever big). He is infinite in power; that's big! He is infinite in wisdom; that's big! He is infinite in knowledge; that's big! I don't think we can begin to imagine just how big He is, but it is fun to think about it.

Genesis 1:1; Nehemiah 9:6;
Jeremiah 10:6; Psalm 86:8

11

Question:

How does God get His power? Where does He get it from?

Miroslava M.

Age 8—Mexico

12

Answer:

Ah, Lord GOD! Behold, You have made the heavens and the earth by Your great power and outstretched arm. There is nothing too hard for You... (Jeremiah 32:17).

We hear a lot about God's power. Take a look at our verse. God's almighty power made the heavens and the earth and there is nothing too hard for God. Well, I want you to learn another big word . . . omnipotent. The Bible clearly teaches that God is omnipotent, meaning He is all powerful. He is Almighty God, He is Lord, the Creator of all things, and He never gets tired! There is none like God. Although we can't completely understand His power, we know He is infinite in power (meaning there is no way to measure it), and all power ultimately comes from Him and the source of His power never becomes exhausted. God can do anything He wants whenever He wants, and nothing is impossible for Him. I am so glad that I serve a God who is all powerful!

Psalm 147:5; Nehemiah 9:6; Mark 10:27

Question: Does God laugh?

Alec P.

Age 10 — Idaho, USA

Answer:

The LORD laughs at him, for He sees that his day is coming (Psalm 37:13).

Well, Alec, we were created in God's image, which means that although we don't look like God, we are like God in other ways. God created us to be able to do things that animals can't do. For example, think, write, read, play games, and laugh! I believe that all of the special things we can do as humans reflect a part of who God is. After all, the Bible tells us that God does have emotions. The Bible tells us about times when God was sad (during Noah's day) and when God is happy (when we obey His Word). So yes, God can laugh with joy.

The Bible also tells us about times when God laughs in a different way at foolish people because they think they can do things against Him. They think they can sin, reject God, and ignore His Word. God laughs at these wicked people, not to be mean, but because He knows that in the end He is the only true and perfect God and He will have the last say—and He judges wickedness.

*Genesis 1:27; Isaiah 62:5; Psalm 2:4;
Proverbs 1:26; Psalm 16:11*

15

Question: How does God know something before it happens?

Trent C.

Answer:

But, beloved, do not forget this one thing, that with the Lord one day is as a thousand years, and a thousand years as one day (2 Peter 3:8).

You know, Trent, the Bible tells us that God is outside of time—to Him a day is like a thousand years, and a thousand years are like a day. He therefore knows everything before it happens. He even created time. He is not bound by time and He sees all of life and history from start to finish at the same time! In other words, He sees the end from the beginning. He sees what is past and what is still to come. The Bible confirms this through the prophets (people in the Bible who told about things that hadn't happened yet). God used these people to let others know some of the things that were going to happen. One example is the Prophet Micah who wrote about Jesus being born long before it happened. Today, God still knows exactly what is going on. He is always doing what pleases Him, and what is best for us, AND He knows all things before they happen! He is truly a great and wonderful God, deserving of our worship and praise!

Genesis 1:1; Isaiah 46:9-10;
Micah 5:2-4; Psalm115:3

Question:

How could God be Jesus and Jesus be God? How can they be the same, but different?

Nancy K.

Age 8— Indiana, USA

18

Answer:

In the beginning was the Word, and the Word was with God, and the Word was God. He was in the beginning with God. All things were made through Him (John 1:1-3).

You are wondering about a very important teaching from the Bible. But there is more here—the Holy Spirit. God is three distinct persons—Father, Son, and Holy Spirit—and each is fully God, yet there is only one God. This is especially hard for us to understand. But remember, God is not like anything else in the whole world.

This might help you to understand a little. In the first chapter of the Bible, God says, "In the beginning God". Now there are some very smart people who study the Bible. These people tell us that the way the word "God" is used here means more than one person. As we read Genesis, we learn that God's Spirit was there at creation, that God Himself spoke all of creation into existence, and Jesus is called the Creator. He is the Creator, and the One who stepped into history and became a man. He did this to help us know God better and to show us how we could one day be with God the Father, God the Son, and God the Holy Spirit. Nancy, because we are created in God's image, we are like Him in some ways—we can think abstractly, love, have relationships and so on. But there are many things very different from us that are hard to understand, and these make God who He is—He is eternal, and He is the triune God. He is one but more than one.

Deuteronomy 6:4; Colossians 1:16; John 1:1

Question: Is the Holy Spirit even with God?

Taylor B.

Age 7— Kansas, USA

Answer:

"And I will pray the Father, and He will give you another Helper, that He may abide with you forever…" (John 14:16).

Taylor, we assume you are asking is the Holy Spirit equal with God. Well, there is only one God, but there are three persons in one God—the Father, the Son, and the Holy Spirit. Because we are not anything like God, this is a mystery that is very hard to understand. The answer to your question is, yes, the Holy Spirit is even (equal) with God because the Holy Spirit IS God. You see, after Jesus (God the Son) died on the cross, He was buried, and He rose from the dead. He did this so that you could have eternal life with Him if you trust in Him and believe in Him. After Jesus rose from the dead, He did something very special for all of us. See our Bible verse above? It says that Jesus sends a Helper, who comes from the Father, who is the Spirit of truth. Jesus sent this Helper to everyone who believes in Him. This Helper (the Holy Spirit) stays with us. He teaches us to pray. He helps us to understand the Bible. He even helps us to love and help other people (even when they don't love us back!) The Holy Spirit is even with God . . . but He stays with us in our heart so that we have help to obey God even when that seems really, really hard!

John 15:26

21

Question: Why can't I hear God talking to me?

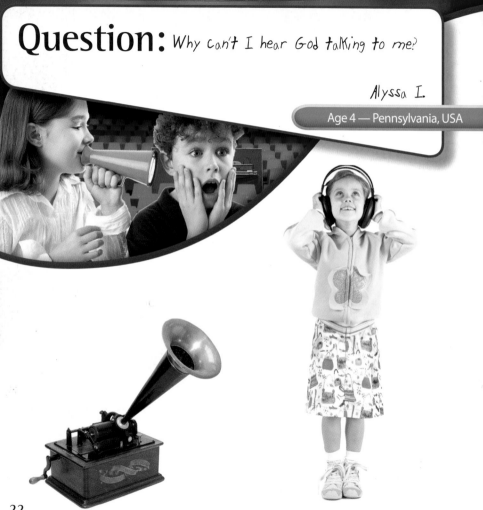

Alyssa I.

Age 4 — Pennsylvania, USA

22

Answer:

God, who at various times and in various ways spoke in time past to the fathers by the prophets, has in these last days spoken to us by His Son . . . (Hebrews 1:1-2).

So, Alyssa, you can't actually "hear" God, right? Well, our verse tells us that long ago, before the Bible was ever printed, God did speak to people. He spoke so they would know what He wanted and so they would know Him. He only spoke to those people He chose and they shared God's words with the others. But you see, those people way back then did not have the Bible, God's written word. We are so blessed to have God's Word. It is like a long letter from God. This letter is like other letters you might get from your mom, grandma, or a friend. When you read a letter, you know that someone is "talking" to you, don't you? It is the same with the Bible. We don't need to hear God out loud because we can "hear" what He has to say by reading the Bible. We think it might be easier if God would just speak out loud and then we would know what He wanted. But He promises that if we study His word we will get to know Him. We need to read it and study it. We need to trust it. When we do that, we WILL hear God through His Word!

2 Timothy 3:16-17; Proverbs 30:5-6

Question:

How do we know that God really answers prayers? Couldn't it be just a coincidence?

McKenzie D.

Age 8 —Tennessee, USA

Answer:

But you, when you pray, go into your room, and when you have shut your door, pray to your Father who is in the secret place; and your Father who sees in secret will reward you openly (Matthew 6:6).

First of all, there are no coincidences with God because He always works all things together according to His plan. He is in charge of everything and His plans always work out. God does answer prayers— and He wants us to pray. He told us to pray and He told us how to pray. I don't believe He would do that if He wasn't going to listen and answer! Jesus Himself prayed to God the Father a lot while He was on earth. Remember that God doesn't always answer prayer the way we think He should. There are times when we see a wonderful answer to prayer really quickly. Then there are times when it might take years of praying before God answers. There are also times when we may never see God's answer to a special prayer. And we need to understand that sin affects our prayers. Sometimes without realizing it or being willing to admit it we pray selfishly for things we shouldn't! We need to continually pray the Lord will show us His Will for our lives. He wants us to pray, He wants us to praise Him in our prayers, and He wants us to ask Him to meet our needs. Praying is talking to God as though He were a very good friend . . . He likes hearing from you that way, so keep it up—He will answer! But He will always answer in the way that He knows is best for us.

Romans 8:28; Job 42:2;
Mark 1:35; Hebrews 11:6

Question: Why did God create sin?

Eddy R.

Age 11 — New Hampshire, US

OK, I
ADMIT IT..
HE DID IT!

26

Answer:

Therefore, just as through one man sin entered the world, and death through sin, and thus death spread to all men, because all sinned (Romans 5:12).

Sin is an action or thought that is in disobedience to God. God created all the heavens and all the earth. He created birds, dinosaurs, the oceans, the earth, the stars, everything including you and me and all people! But He did NOT create sin. When God created people, He knew we would disobey Him—though He created Adam and Eve with the potential to sin. And when Adam and Eve sinned (disobeyed God) in the Garden, the Bible tells us that in Adam the whole human race sinned and fell. Now this is the really amazing part! God uses our sin to show how loving, just, and merciful He is to us. You see, it is because of our sin that God stepped into history to be a man—Jesus—to die on the cross, to be raised from the dead, and to be saved from the punishment for sin. God shows us how much He loves us by forgiving our sins and giving us a way to get to heaven. If we believe in Him and trust Him as Lord of our lives, we will go to heaven because Jesus took the punishment for our sin. So, we are to blame for sin not God. But because of our sin, God wants to save us and show us the most amazing love He has for us. He is a wonderful God!

Romans 3:23; Romans 6:23; John 3:16

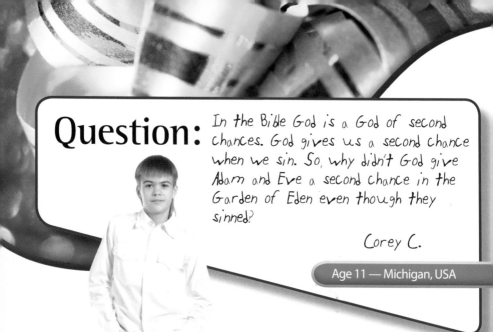

Question:

In the Bible God is a God of second chances. God gives us a second chance when we sin. So, why didn't God give Adam and Eve a second chance in the Garden of Eden even though they sinned?

Corey C.

Age 11 — Michigan, USA

Answer:

For by grace you have been saved through faith, and that not of yourselves; it is the gift of God, not of works, lest anyone should boast (Ephesians 2:8-9).

First of all, let's take a look at the word "chance." Chance means that something just happened; that it wasn't planned. Nothing happens by "chance" because God knows everything. He doesn't give us a second chance. He gives us a FREE GIFT—forgiveness through Jesus! When Adam and Eve sinned the whole creation fell—it was no longer perfect! Nothing humans could do could undo that. Adam and Eve were sent out of the Garden. But they continued to live on earth, have children, and teach their children and grandchildren all about God and His mercy. I believe that when God killed that very first animal and gave Adam and Eve clothes to wear, He was sharing a picture of the gospel, the message of salvation with them. He was helping them to understand that it would take a perfect sacrifice to take away the sins of all people and that perfect sacrifice would be God Himself—Jesus Christ. Everyone who believes in Jesus Christ as Lord and Savior will receive the free gift of eternal life in heaven. Adam and Eve were dead in their sins and so are we. God gave us something far better than a "second chance." What we do get is a free gift if we will receive it by believing and trusting in Jesus Christ.

Job 42:2; Romans 11:36; Acts 4:12

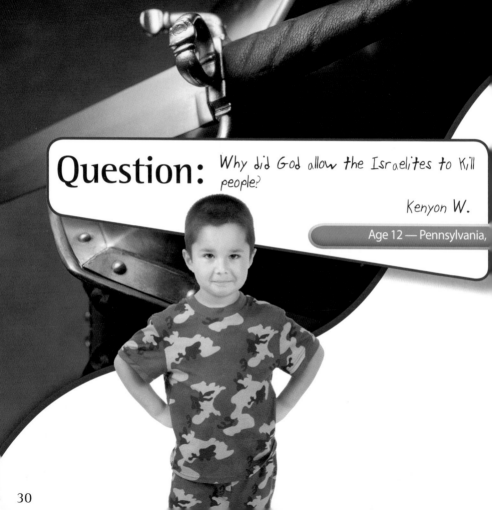

Question: Why did God allow the Israelites to kill people?

Kenyon W.

Age 12 — Pennsylvania,

30

Answer:

Then the LORD saw that the wickedness of man was great in the earth, and that every intent of the thoughts of his heart was only evil continually (Genesis 6:5).

Our verse from Genesis tells us two very important things—that people of the earth were wicked and that God knows all the thoughts and intents of man's heart. It seems like the Israelites killed innocent people. But we need to learn a couple of things here. First, there are no innocent people . . . the Bible clearly says that we ALL have sinned against a holy and just God. Second, God did not only allow the Israelites to kill the people, He commanded them to do it. Because God is holy, He needs to judge sin and wickedness. He used the Israelites to judge the people and remove the evil in the land. We know there are still evil, wicked people today. But God doesn't command us to destroy those people in the same way. That is because Jesus Christ died on the cross. God judged the sin in the world by punishing His Son on the cross. The Bible tells us that God Himself will judge those who do not claim Jesus Christ as their Savior--those who do not receive Jesus' free gift of forgiveness and who refuse to trust Him and believe in Him as the one and only way to heaven.

Deuteronomy 9:1-4; Psalm 14:2-3;
2 Peter 3:7; Romans 10:13

HOLY BIBLE

Question: Why did God create us?

Joy B.

Age 11 — Michigan, USA

32

Answer:

For of Him and through Him and to Him [are] all things, to whom [be] glory forever. Amen. (Romans 11:36)."

Many, many people, young and old, have asked similar questions. What is my purpose? Why did God create me? The answer is very simple and very clear in the Bible. God created us to glorify Him and to enjoy Him forever. We were created by Him and for Him. He did not need us because He was lonely or wanted someone to talk to. God is perfect and complete and has always been that way. We belong completely to Him. Because of that, we are to glorify Him in everything that we do. How do we do that? We love Him, obey Him, believe in Jesus Christ, trust in Jesus, receiving the free gift Jesus offers us . . . only then will we give glory to God, and only then we will be able to enjoy Him forever, for all eternity!

Zephaniah 3:17; 1 Corinthians 10:31;
1 Peter 4:11

33

Question: How did the authors of the Bible know what all God did during the creation, since there was no one to see what He did, how do we know what really happened?

Annabel H.

Age 7 — Alabama, USA

Answer:

God is not a man, that He should lie . . .(Numbers 23:19).

Let's see, Annabel. There are people who believe in evolution who think that billions of years ago (when no one was there to see) the universe came into existence by a big bang. Then billions of years ago (when no one was there to see) the earth came into existence. Then billions of years ago (when no one was there to see) life formed on earth. Then millions of years ago (still no one there to see!) animals began changing into other animals. Then two million years ago (yep, still no one there!) an animal like an ape began to change into a human being. That's their story . . . but there wasn't anyone around to see it. Well, guess what? In the Bible we are told that God has given His word to men to write down so we can know how everything came to be. The Bible, which is God's Word, though penned by man, tells us that God WAS there and He has given us an eyewitness account of exactly how the universe and everything in it was created. The Bible tells us thousands of times that it is the Word of God. My questions to you is, "Do you trust God, who knows everything, who has always been there, who never changes, and who doesn't tell a lie OR a human being who doesn't know everything, changes his mind, changes his story, and wasn't always there?" Well, I believe God and that makes real sense!

Malachi 3:6; Luke 21:33;
Genesis 1:1

HOLY
BIBLE

35

Question: Where did the Bible come from?

Allison R.

Answer:

. . . for prophecy never came by the will of man, but holy men of God spoke as they were moved by the Holy Spirit (2 Peter 1:21).

Look at our verse above. It says that the Bible came from holy men of God. These men were inspired by God through the Holy Spirit working in their hearts. There were about 40 different writers over a very long time who wrote the Bible. They were from many different life styles—like a doctor, a farmer, and even a fisherman. Just like there were different people, there are different types of writing, like history, poetry, and prophecy (which tells about the future). The amazing thing about the Bible is that even though so many people wrote it over such a long time, it has just one message, it tells one story, and it points to one person, Jesus Christ our Lord and Savior. There is no other book like it on this earth. And if you are called by God, His words will be the joy and the delight of your heart!

2 Timothy 3:16; Psalm 119:89;
Proverbs 30:5-6; Matthew 4:4

Question: How did God communicate with Moses?

Krystianna L.

Age 8 — California, USA

MAIL

38

Answer:

So the LORD spoke to Moses face to face, as a man speaks to his friend. . . . (Exodus 33:11).

Can you imagine it? Speaking to God? Look at our verse. It says that the LORD spoke to Moses as a man speaks to his friend. How wonderful that must have been. Actually, the Bible tells us that God spoke out loud to Moses many times as he led the Israelites to the Promised Land. God wanted to be sure the people knew exactly what He expected of them. It must have been incredible for Moses because we read in Exodus that after God spoke to Moses his face would shine bright. I believe that the Bible's account of God speaking to Moses is one of the many wonderful, miraculous things we read about in the Bible. The shining face of Moses also reminds us of how holy God is!

Exodus 33:20-23; Exodus 3:4;
Exodus 19:19

Question:

Just why is the Bible true? I believe but I just don't understand why it's true.

Bennett F.

Age 9 — Kentucky, USA

40

Answer:

All Scripture is given by inspiration of God, and is profitable for doctrine, for reproof, for correction, for instruction in righteousness… (2 Timothy 3:16).

The Bible is no ordinary book for many reasons. Paul in his letter to Timothy tells us that the Bible is God's "inspired" Word. In fact, in the original Greek language of the New Testament, the word "inspired" really means that the words of the Bible have been "breathed out" by God through the men who wrote them down. If the Bible is from God, we would expect it to be true and we should be able to test it. We can do this in many ways. In Genesis chapters 1 – 11 we can read an account of many historical events concerning the beginning of this world. Through application of science we can confirm that God's account of creation is true. As an example, God tells us in Genesis chapter 1 that animals, plants, birds, fish, and every living thing were created after their own kind (dogs only produce dogs, etc.). This is exactly what we observe. We are also able to confirm many other aspects of the Bible's history in other areas of science such as geology and astronomy. We can also rely on the Bible's truth concerning Jesus—for instance, in considering how many prophecies about Him were made hundreds of years before He came to earth as a man. Because we can confirm the history in the Bible, we can have faith in all that the Bible has to say. However, the main reason we can trust the Bible is because it is from God—which is different from every other book on earth. Thus we should use the Bible as the starting point for all our living, learning, and actions.

2 Corinthians 5:17; 2 Peter 1:20, 21;
Colossians 1:16-17; John 14:6

41

Question: Why is it that whenever I mention anything about the Bible in school I get into trouble?.

Carynn B.

Age 9 — Illinois, USA

42

Answer:

I have given them Your word; and the world has hated them because they are not of the world, just as I am not of the world (John 17:14).

Jesus gave us His Word and He told us that the world would hate us because of it. If you are a Christian, you are different from the rest of the world. It is a very sad situation here in America that in public schools there is much confusion about God and the Bible, and what people can say or do. Many want to keep "religion" completely out of the schools. But when we try to keep God out of schools we end up teaching the kids that there is no God. They are learning that the universe can be explained without God. Well, that IS a religion. It is the religion of atheism, believing in NO god. I believe that people are afraid of God's Word and they don't want to have anything to do with it. Why? Because to believe God's Word means you allow Him to make all the rules. It means He tells us that we are sinners and He has the right to tell us what is right and wrong. People just don't like being told they are sinners in rebellion against God, and they don't like being told what to do. The Bible warns us that we will be treated badly because we believe in Jesus. We need to know what the Bible says and share it with others so they can see that it is actually a wonderful book, a book of truth that shows us the way to eternal life by believing and trusting in Jesus.

Matthew 12:30; James 4:4;
Romans 8:7; Romans 10:9

43

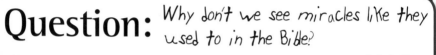

Question: Why don't we see miracles like they used to in the Bible?

Soleil H.

Age 8 — Virginia, USA

Trust in Him!

Believe

44

Answer:

Now these things [such as the miracle of the crossing of the Red Sea] happened to them as an example, and they were written for our instruction… (1 Corinthians 10:11).

Miracles are very special events performed by the power of our almighty, holy God. We read about many miracles in the Bible. In the Old Testament, God used miracles to show the people that He was the ONE true God! He parted the Red Sea, brought terrible plagues, fed the Israelites in the wilderness. In the New Testament, Jesus did miracles as signs so people would know He was the Son of God as He claimed. He walked on water, healed the sick, and even raised the dead! We don't need such signs today as we have God's Word, the Bible. However, God is still a God of miracles today. We all pray for healing from sickness from time to time, either for ourselves or for others. God may or may not give physical healing at that time. The prayer of faith always includes a "but if not" (Dan. 3:18). God changing our hearts from desiring evil to desiring Him IS a wonderful miracle I pray has occurred in your life. God is pleased with our faith as we put our trust in His Word and the miracles written there, given to us as examples to learn about who God is and to obey Him. And when we look at the creation, we are seeing the miracle of life every day! Don't forget, the greatest miracle ever is that God Himself stepped into history as a man, Jesus Christ, and He died, was buried, and rose again! That's the miracle we all need to believe in.

Exodus 7:5; John 11:42;
1 Corinthians 15:3-4

45

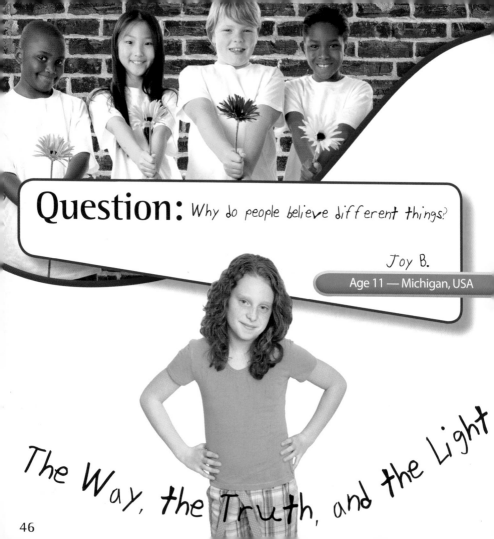

Question: Why do people believe different things?

Joy B.

Age 11 — Michigan, USA

The Way, the Truth, and the Light

Answer:

… who suppress the truth in unrighteousness… (Romans 1:18).

Well, think about it. It was 6000 years ago when the first person decided to believe a truth different from God's. It was in the Garden of Eden—Adam and Eve believed Satan instead of God and they ate the forbidden fruit. When they disobeyed God, they showed us that they wanted to decide their own truth. Since then, men have sinned by ignoring God's truth and believing different things. Our Bible verse tells us they 'suppress the truth'—their heart does not want the true God. People believe so many different things because they are sinners and they don't want to listen to God. The Bible tells us clearly that we must believe God's Word. It tells us that if we don't believe God's Word we will spend eternity separated from Him. My prayer is that you will come to believe the one truth that can save you by putting your faith and trust in the Lord Jesus who is the only way to God the Father and heaven. And you can be sure that if you have any questions about God, Jesus, or how to get to heaven, the Bible will give the answer. It is the true Word of God!

Genesis 2:4-5; Jeremiah 17:9;
John 5:24

47

Answers Are Always Important!

The Answers Book for Kids answers questions from children around the world in this four-volume series. Each volume will answer 22 questions in a friendly and readable style appropriate for children 6–12 years old; and each covers a unique topic including, *Creation and the Fall; Dinosaurs and the Flood of Noah; God and the Bible;* and *Sin, Salvation, and the Christian Life.* Explore:

- Why the first person God created was a boy.

- How Adam named all the animals.

- Why the Bible is true.

- What being "born again" means.